T0345524

These Figures Lining the Hills

ALICE ATTIE

These Figures Lining the Hills

LONDON NEW YORK CALCUTTA

Seagull Books, 2015

Text and images © Alice Attie, 2015

ISBN 978 0 8574 2 304 7

British Library Cataloguing-in-Publication Data
A catalogue record for this book is available from the British Library.

Book designed by Sunandini Banerjee, Seagull Books, Calcutta, India
Printed and bound by Maple Press, York, Pennsylvania, USA

To my precious children, Justine and Gideon

To my loving partner, Royce

To my dear mother, Muriel

It is impossible to say everything,
and it is impossible not to say everything.

Franz Kafka

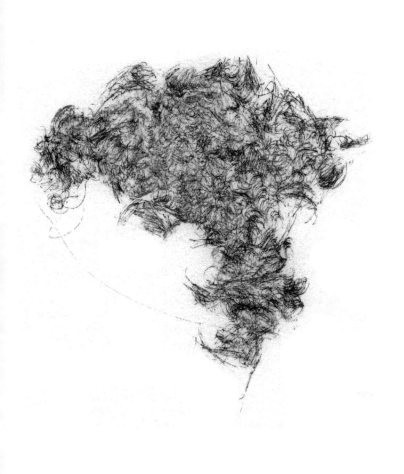

ONE

Words are like pellets of breath.
We breathe them in.

We walk through the grass on a balmy day.
We quicken and slacken our pace.

There is no beginning and no end to writing.
There is no place where it culminates.

The man in the field is written for my gaze.
He projects himself, portraits himself in the landscape.

He is the being that he is.
In the crevices of language, we are wedged.

TWO

I can see him from the window in the form of a figure.
He has the form of a man chopping,
He has the form of a man curved in the curve of his gathering.

I can see him.

His shape forces the mind.
It is subject for the subject of thought.

Language hosts these figures.
They are shapes.

The shape of the man is the shape of the man.

The wind kicks up and sways the world.
Everything in view is in view and nothing more.

THREE

To make a collage of writing, from daybreak to dusk, to chronicle the mind's involutions, to take the bits, fragment by fragment, the inklings, the suppositions, inch by inch, send them out, stamp them, paste them, corner them, toss them, trim them, tangle them, disperse them, raise and lower them, fraction them, cut them in darkness, cut them in light, single and plural them, long for them, find them, first to last, imagine a meaning for them.

FOUR

Drape one over another
one fiction
one fact

Lift
and fold

Take note of it
the smallest thing

What it is
what it does

Take note of it
the smallest thing

FIVE

We learn to speak of it, to roll the cocoon of language around it.
To say what it is—here paper, here book, here pen, here in,
We breathe deeply for the utterance of what is not here.
We hold sounds close, as sighs, pushed and dragged.

We say that we are here.
The pines in winter companion us.
Black night is present to us, here.
We hold its nomination: darkness, constellation, mystery.

One is revealed and another concealed.
We learn this in the conversation of being.
To say what is here, as certainty, as vow.
We learn it and we give it.

We speak it.
Here and here.
When night comes, we huddle in poetry.
We slip into its folds and close the eyes of our tongues

To silence.

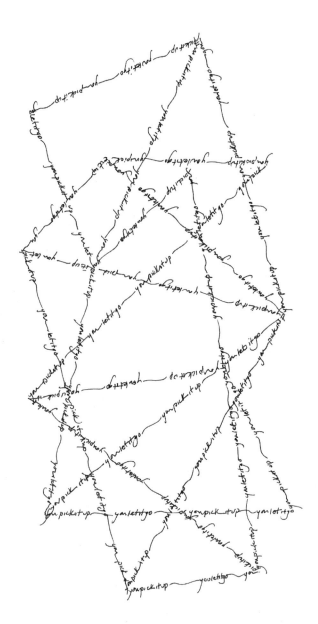

SIX

It begins like weather.
You awake and step into it.

You muse on its subtleties.
The ink spreads its fact to the white attendant page.

Here is where it begins.

Something tumbles to the ground.
You pick it up.

You let it go.
You roll it into the mouth and speak.

SEVEN

someone is speaking   there is a voice   it opens   I step in

I hear it   I see it   as a tree shivers   I see it   shiver in the wind

it folds   it opens   as a branch in the light   it shivers   it opens

as a footstep to the soil   it seeps in   I find it   I feel it

I take note of it

as leaves   acknowledge light   I acknowledge it

I see it   as a voice

it rises   in curvatures   in forms

it whispers the leaves   shivers the light

I hear murmurs   I write them   they line up

as figures   they are conjugated

as filaments they are set down   they come   as speech comes

as writing comes

as the light speaks   move closer   you can hear it   move closer

as the light translates the leaves   you can see it

you can rise into it

you can shiver into the transparencies

they will lift and carry you

here you can   hear them speaking   they tremble   as I write

where it swells   where it leans   into silence

where it leans into speech

into light   I name it   I turn it   here

can you hear it   can you   can you hear the ooze of speech

rhythming the light   hear   where you are

where a fistful of words   dangles

as the spider from her web dangles   climbs the light

ask why it shivers   why it dangles   why it murmurs

as noon in a day murmurs

ask what can it be   that hangs in the bellied air

slips into it   what can it be   that conjugates the light

EIGHT

She takes the pen to page. She does so again and again. She watches writing take shape, sentences lean to the right, ideas lean to the left. She lets a mistaken word become the kernel of a thought that differs from the one she set out to write. She abhors the messy page, the cross-outs, the sullying. Each day she begins again. Sometimes, she takes a sentence from a book she is reading. Each sentence works. The beauty of any sentence impresses her.

Sentences from Gilles Deleuze's essay 'Literature and Life':

> *There are no straight lines, neither in things nor in language. Syntax is the set of necessary detours that are created in each case to reveal the life of things.*[1]

> *Literature begins only when a third person is born in us that strips us of the power to say 'I'.*[2]

She invents the third person of herself.

She enumerates the valences,
Numbers them,
Lifts and carries them,

She seeks in the spaces between them,
Not the missing persons but the hidden ones.

NINE

Thinking of Borges Thinking of Spinoza

Because all things long to exist in their beings.
Because silence longs for deeper silence.
Because all things long to exist.
Because this small creature is inexorably here.
Because it holds firmly to its being.
Because not being is the possibility of being gone.
Because being longs for absence.
Because such knowledge exists.
Because not one but many is being here.
Because many long to exist.
Because sounds cling in time.
Because each utterance persists in being.
Because each is a plural in the guise of one.
Because plural is the singular event of being.
Because all things long to exist in being.

TEN

To speak is to place a stone in the landscape.
Words are like stones.

We search for them.

We are sucked in.
We fall and are sucked in.

We slip into crevices and drop down.
To dwell in the unspoken, and in the effort,

We pick words to rub against.

We marvel at myriad spoken tongues,
Regrets, laments, exultations.

ELEVEN

We have chosen the meaning
Of being numerous

Each a particular
Each a numeral

O for this thing
O for the marking of it

O is a stone
O is obdurate

O is the diction of stoneness
O the silence of it

The hard fact of it
The lost and found of it

Plumb and weight
O

TWELVE

Why is there being instead of nothing?

Why
is
there
something
instead of
nothing
?

We cannot speak of nothing.

The children are out to play.
I see them.
In the late afternoon,
I hear
Their muffled song lift the air.
I hear
It.

I write it down.
I mark it.
I take note.

O takes the place of X.

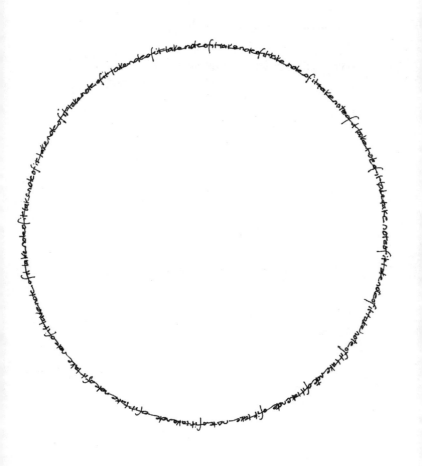

THIRTEEN

A loon calls from the heart of the lake.

The countertenor takes it further.

FOURTEEN

Wet rain beads the trees
Limbs drop their heavy loads
A punctuated rhythm

this is this is this

You trudge the woods on slow feet
You are moving into it
You hear groaning and moaning

You think of Benjy running towards the fence

bellowing

You are here

Up to your ears in
This exact moment

You are here

this is this is this

Bellows in the cave of the ear

FIFTEEN

For Benjy, there is no fiction and there are no facts.
For Vardaman, we pull the outside in; we push the inside out.

My mother is a fish.

We name a place that is no place.
We cross because Benjy cannot.

We say *fish* and *fish* and *fish*.

SIXTEEN

It is like an engine.
The sound of an animal in distress
Is like an engine.

Your metaphors are stuck.
Engine is all you have.

The sound comes closer.
You seek shelter.
You disappear into the fear of it.

SEVENTEEN

All night, all morning,
We listen to stories.

This flower has no name.
It flows like blood.

A fustian anatomy.

EIGHTEEN

Like pulling a thread, the hem unravels but a fold remains to remind you. Like falling asleep as the name of someone you love escapes you. Like a back door that stays open awaiting a visitation. It's like that, on the cusp of it, on the very edge.

It is as a tourist arrives in the train station. There are signs everywhere and she is unsure. A clue rises up. She follows a small crowd in a direction marked by a large green exit sign. Exit, she thinks, is a start. She walks into the air. It is heavy with foreignness. She walks into it and takes note. The cars seem smaller than she remembers. Here, near the station, people linger, strange and familiar at the same time.

In the afternoon, she walks out from the small hotel onto the narrow street. There are cranes pulling up the cobblestones. An effort to rearrange them, she imagines, perhaps a lost civilization, all this digging. She shifts her attention to the windows, to the advertisements and to a man sweeping the street. There are layers that are hidden, lost to the immediacy of experience.

Think forward, she reminds herself, walk; for the plan is to trace her steps backwards, to assure a return to this place. Her thoughts come and go: what it means to be lost, how one would wrestle out of being lost.

She traces it, takes note of it, fixes it in the mind—this narrowness, these machines working, the rubble that piles up, the names written and the certainty of being here, now, in the event of tracing. The world is like this. Foreign and familiar. The face one meets may return—it may stare into something you will call memory. I will see that face one day; it will come to me when I recall myself to this strangeness, to a sensation I had wandering in a place both foreign and familiar.

She remembers Camus, in his journal, remarking that one does not travel for pleasure. One travels for fear. Maybe, she thinks, this is fear.

In a small room opening onto a small street a small rain taps a small tune. She contemplates the hours as they move in small regular increments, as sure as anything she has ever known.

There is still time to see it all, to take it in, to let the weight of this otherness descend, incite her imagination to centuries past, perhaps to the sounds of footsteps, to writing in small places, in small rooms, secluded and alone.

She thinks of the great museum. She could walk into a room in the great museum, gaze at a painting and be drawn in. She could look at a kitchen scene, the woman's skirt pulled up just slightly, bands of light raking through the small window, the bread dark, the wood table darker, the baskets that carry knives—she could think it out. She could come to some conclusion about it. She could draw a line, connect it to something, step back and forth, into and out of it. She could do that in the great museum.

If she traces the line from there to here, she could expand the smallness, give everything heft, place herself in the largesse of it. The world is essential, she thinks, just as it is. This small room is essential, small within the larger planet. The large planet is small, small within the larger universe. Essential, all.

She thinks about these things and anticipates a kind of certainty, moving from the small kitchen in the painting to the small street in the small town in the large world. She traces a thin fold on an imagined fabric and she comprehends it. The small room—she comprehends it as it is. Time and the weight of it. Place and the weight of it. Fear and the event of it. The lines. Essential. Essential, all of it.

NINETEEN

Who was he who
showed up briefly in the morning to
reappear in the photograph on the bookshelf
who was he gone but whispering in the crook of the ear
a distance a nearness something
trembling as a slip of memory lifts the veil of it
knocks on the door of it rounds the corner of it
breaks it pounds into the powder of it
pulsing the air hung with images shivering
sounding seeing hearing they come towards one
they circle they dip they rise one and then another
who was he who showed in the half-light
half-wholly there to touch to look at
something in the face or the belly of it
who was he who teased the half-sight
flickering visible invisible almost
poised to jimmy himself up to lean on and
be cinched as a dream is cinched as
subject in the object of the room is cinched
as candescence and shadow are and were and will be
never again who was he who stood at the door
a silence repeating an absence a million times
she called a million images in the morning faded

TWENTY

leaves
are falling

birds
are falling

these named
fluttering things

fall

as gingko
falls

as wren
falls

as
we

swallow

as
we

pine

these named
fluttering things

fall

TWENTY-ONE

let them spill over
let them seep down
let them muffle in the mouth
let them fall against its walls
let them be wind in the throat
let them scratch against the mind
let them hand themselves over
let them tangle
let them be and not be

TWENTY-TWO

Line them up
like vowels
a and *o* and *u*

Count birds on a wire
count seashells

      one
      two
      three

Like pebbles
they spill from the mouth

a small steady tumbling

TWENTY-THREE

The days. They curl. They spread. They vanish.
One after the other, the good days and the lesser days, the years.

one two three four five six seven eight nine ten eleven twelve
thirteen fourteen fifteen sixteen seventeen eighteen nineteen
twenty twenty-one twenty-two twenty-three twenty-four
twenty-five twenty-six twenty-seven twenty-eight twenty-nine
thirty thirty-one thirty-two thirty-three thirty-four thirty-five
thirty-six thirty-seven thirty-eight thirty-nine forty forty-one
forty-two forty-three forty-four forty-five forty-six forty-seven
forty-eight forty-nine fifty fifty-one fifty-two fifty-three fifty-
four fifty-five fifty-six fifty-seven fifty-eight fifty-nine sixty
sixty-one sixty-two sixty-three sixty-four sixty-five

1234567891011121314151617181920212223242526272829303132
3334353637383940414243444546474849505152535455565758596
06162636465

The years have no boundaries.
They slide over one another.

We take note.

TWENTY-FOUR

You walk in to the night as you walk into stories. You think of black, of fear, more naked than death, more capable, more visceral.

You walk past landmarks. You phrase them.
You touch the thickness of trees, walking close to them, rubbing against them, asking in a low voice.

Your memories are stones placed in a field.
You lay them in the sun. You turn them.
You think through them.
You select and hold them up to the light.

Beethoven and the sonata, Kant and the limits of reason, the stones on the Cathedral of St John the Divine, stonemasons, the coffee shop, writing in public spaces, beer in the windows of the bodega, sitting on the stoop talking about it, reading troubadour poets, Bach's Mass in B minor, Beethoven's Missa Solemnis, Martin Buber, the reciprocal.

You walk in to the night as you walk into stories. You think of black, of fear, more naked than death, more capable, more visceral.

You walk past landmarks. You phrase them.
You touch the thickness of trees, walking close to them,
rubbing against them, asking in a low voice.

You wait for the lights to change.
They blink through small slits in the world's darkness.
You think of light, of telling stories,
Of leaving nothing behind.

TWENTY-FIVE

Louise Bourgeois is seated at a small table. A small light dims a small room. Sennelier inks on the mantle make me think of Barthes, his neutral grey. Louise is not neutral. She exudes opinion. She opens and closes down. We are seated in a circle around a small table. Our works are in our laps. We wait to show her, each in our turn. It is early in the day. A bottle of whiskey sits on the table, in the centre, surrounded by small paper cups. It is early for this offering, I think to myself. A recent graduate reads a short story aloud to us. It is silly. I feel embarrassed by his awkwardness. He has also brought a pogo stick to show Louise, a strange contraption with things hanging from one end. He is young. A woman reads a poem in a language that none of us understand; it is something about love and Louise and Mother's Day. I am not convinced. The room feels cluttered. It is my turn; I bring out two large text drawings and place them on the too-small table in front of her; the dim light barely illuminates them. She compliments the work in a soft voice. Then, the doorbell rings and there is a sudden shuffling of positions. A man, with long unkempt hair, and a woman enter; he towers over our cramped gathering and places a box of chocolates in front of Louise. It is her son. She quietly pushes the chocolates to the side.

Mother's Day

TWENTY-SIX

In the grammar of pain
I am separate.

Pain is yellow.
Pain is blue.

Mine is mine.
Yours is you.

TWENTY-SEVEN

With a series of fragments written over a few months, Roland Barthes mourned his mother's death.

Journal de deuil

On small strips of paper, there are small bits of language, small possibilities.

Each of us has his own rhythm of suffering.[3]

The tiny offerings issue forth.

I don't want to talk about it, for fear of making literature out of it.
Although as a matter of fact, literature originates within these truths.[4]

Death of the mother = death of love = death of language

Did Barthes once say that language was a skin you touch, you rub against?
He touches the skin-language; touches it, like a kiss.

Loss comes back as tiny pieces, as fragments.
Fragments collage into a book.

Maybe something valuable in these notes.[5]

The binding of the book = the binding of what is left to say

> *My suffering is* inexpressible *but all the same* utter-
> able, *speakable.*[6]

The sighs of language are small stones placed on the heart.

TWENTY-EIGHT

We invent it for ourselves. We name it land and sea and sky.
We divide its reaches
arbitrarily into degrees of latitude and longitude,
supplemented by a contrivance we call time.
We keep ourselves in orderly fashion
by imposing on it grids entirely of our own.
We forget, because we have to in order to endure our plight,
that these are rationales of own logic.[7]

Anne Truitt

TWENTY-NINE

Midday.
Clouds hang their grey bags across the sky.
The air swells in heat.

Elsewhere
Clouds hang like pain,
Heavy and dark.

Elsewhere
Panic gathers like
Crickets in the noonday sun.

It is summer,
Peak for the opulence of nature's purse.

The heart pushes into its cavities.
Thunder rolls its giant voice,
Summoning a strange elegance.

Disasters
Hang too.

Like hives
She remembers

Like hives
They hang in hell.

THIRTY

The red-eyed cicadas cry out in the landscape.
The brood will mate and then die.

Every 17 years

From the mist-cloaked trees,
mating calls grow to a deafening din.
They rise and fall, again and again and again.
Like rolling waves,
scratching and howling in a steady rhythm.

Yesterday, the keeper of the cemetery came by to talk. His
wife died last week of a cancer that raged rapidly through
her unsuspecting body. Grief. The enormity of her absence
was like the rise of a wave, cresting in the cavity of his heart.
He said he didn't know what all this noise in the landscape
was. He thought the world was crying.

I arrange bodies of dead cicadas in a box.
The spectacle has ended.
In their deaths, red drains from their eyes. I line them up
and pin them.

1 2 3 4 5 6 7 8 9 10 11 12 13 14 15 16 17

The world will have a new history.

bvizbozbizbvibbozbizbvizbozbizbvibbozbizbvibbozbizbvibbozbizbvibbozbizbvibbozbizbvibbozbizbvibbozbizbvibbozbizbvibbozbizbvibbozbizbvibbozbizbvibbozbizbvibbozbizbvibbozbiz

zigzagging zigzagging

THIRTY-ONE

Spiders.

We walk into their webs.
We crash into them and keep walking.

We do.
We destroy and keep going.

For there is no end to it.

There are 400,000 species of beetle
among the estimated 1.5 million species of insect.
Elaborate patterns and colours for predacious eyes.
There are 10 quintillion insects:
nineteen zeros after the number one.

A tiny insect makes its way across the table.

Lugging its loot, it lumbers, fragile and distracted,

      Zigzagging.

I blow; it squats and quakes and, suddenly, lifts and flies off.

I open my mouth. It will fly in and feel the cavern of my throat.
I imagine a mouthful, in the quantity of quintillion.

I shrink.
I consider my figure, on extended legs,

Zigzagging.

A distracted wind unsteadies us. Rocks us.
We skitter and are snuffed out.

This is all that there is.

Quintillion possibilities for the writing of it,
for the flight into the throat.

I open my mouth. They fly in and feel the cavern of my throat.
I imagine this in the quantity of quintillion.

THIRTY-TWO

I zigzag
      you zigzag
            we zigzag
                  they zigzag
                       he and she and it zigzag

A wavering.

      To zigzag in a bookstore

Where will we zigzag when all of the bookstores are gone?

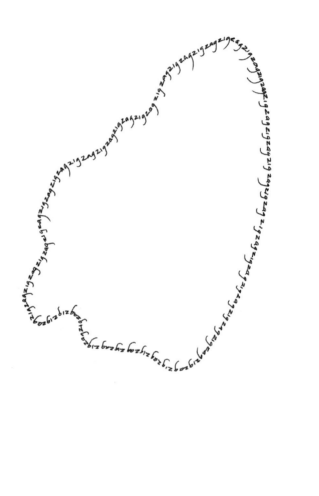

THIRTY-THREE

My astonishment that time—our substance—
can be shared with others.

Jorge Luis Borges

by chance   the day takes hold
by chance   beginnings
by chance   the weight of time
by chance   the timbre
by chance   a bend in history
by chance   this crossing
by chance   the steps taken
by chance   the figures meet on the page
by chance   we have time

THIRTY-FOUR

Adorno says that Kant set up house in the finite world and then explored the house in every direction.

Set up house.

Step into it.

Push against its walls.

THIRTY-FIVE

This room
Think inside it
Push against its walls

See nothing that is not there

THIRTY-SIX

Kant went to bed early every night.
He refused to talk philosophy over meals.
He made his own mustards.
He enjoyed playing billiards.

THIRTY-SEVEN

I select one sentence to think about.

> *For the issue depends on freedom; it is within the power of freedom to pass beyond any and every specified limit.*[8]

I select another.

> *For although the whole of thought could be divided and distributed among many subjects,*
> *the subjective 'I' can never be divided and distributed,*
> *and it is this 'I' that we presuppose in all thinking.*[9]

THIRTY-EIGHT

I ride the N train to 23rd street.

I order soup.
The couple next to me orders soup.
We all order soup.

THIRTY-NINE

The young man hated the film I thought was brilliant.
What it all means.

FORTY

But perhaps the answer that stands closest to my heart
is something else:
Think what it would be
to have a work conceived from outside the self,
a work that would let us escape the limited perspective
of the individual ego,
not only to enter into selves like our own but to give speech to that
which has no language, to the bird perching on the edge of the gutter,
to the tree in spring and the tree in fall, to stone . . .[10]

Italo Calvino

FORTY-ONE

crickets
are small
she thinks

click
and
click
and
click

they gather
in conflux

they amass
in collusion

pile
one
on top of
the other

one
and
two
and

three
they burst in
trios and tremolos

like this

she thinks
precisely

like that
she thinks

and
that
and
that

FORTY-TWO

It falls to one or the other to do the mimicking,
Monarch for pleasure. Viceroy for pain.

Maybe name them
Lovers.

Bring tongues to the tips of wings.
Write the page orange.

Light it with
Small fires.

Flood the mouth.
Taste it.

Maybe burn it,
Like hunger.

FORTY-THREE

Inside the yellowing day is the yellowing mind.
Caterpillars crossing the road
Intermittently stop to reconsider
The palpable tastes of October.

Our words tell orange and red.
They tell of the yellowing of the world.

For here, an insect dressed as a stick
Wanders in broad daylight,
Pincers poised to pick a prey
To fill his leanest body.

Our words tell orange and red.
They tell of the yellowing of the world.

We search these hirsute names for
A brown furry thing—call it woolly bear
Before the inner moth
Takes flight—call it dressed for mimicry.

Imagine them,
Dangling for our intuition.

We close our eyes
As the curtain is drawn,
As shadows hover,
As darkness drops down.

Our words tell orange and red,
They tell of the yellowing of the world.

FORTY-FOUR

The mind skips from clarity to vagueness.
Everything that enters becomes something else.

FORTY-FIVE

Open books randomly, pluck a sentence, maybe a phrase.
Walter Benjamin collected quotations, savoured them,
saved them in notebooks.

All sentences are stunning.

Gems. Great and lesser gems. Pieces and wholes,
take them one by one.
Build something.

Experiment in culling. Le Clézio, Flannery O'Connor,
Daniel on Foucault, Rilke, Borges, Deleuze, Plato, Adorno,
Pound, Foucault, Gombrowicz.

> *And always there were houses, beige walls, gardens,*
> *trees in the wind.*[11]

> *He ran down the steps to where the blind man was,*
> *and stopped.*[12]

> *He seemed a kind of frail samurai, gnarled, dry,*
> *hieratic, with bleached eyebrows,*
> *a slightly sulfurous charm, and an avid and affable*
> *curiosity intriguing to everyone.*[13]

Just this.
I am a cowardly man.[14]

This is the nature of the associate or adjacent space:
each statement is inseparable via
certain rules of change (vectors.)[15]

Very true.

However, he himself does not perceive it in that light;
a dialectical way of seeing is quite
foreign to him.[16]

Even the grey pack knew me and knew fear.[17]

Turning one's gaze on the self means turning it away
from others first of all.[18]

Again silence, the meadow, azure, the sun already
lower, shadows spreading.[19]

FORTY-SIX

NYC. Saturday. Stay in to do some writing, some drawing. Good to stay in.

I work, break, organize, return to the drawing page, write, make lists, arrange the lists, do laundry, eat lunch, think about the next book, glance at the newspaper, write an email to Gideon, a text to Justine, review the coming week on the calendar, call my mom, fiddle around with the radio, find Saturday afternoon at the opera, help her tune in, remind myself to pick up a copy of Sebald's *Rings of Saturn* for Royce, remind myself to reread it, take notes next time, walk more, like Sebald, walk more and take note, maybe photograph more, maybe not, put air in the bicycle tires, get ready in case the weather breaks, remember to talk to Carter about all things concerning June, try to find a German edition of Kafka's parables for Robert, wonder whether Robert will think them too dark, think about Kafka's moodiness, wonder about my attraction to the diaries and the letters, his awkwardness, his suffering, think about the lost art of letter writing, the event of emailing, texting, think about the virtues and misfortunes of brevity and speed, wonder if I will meet my goal of writing more, sort out the diversions, try to minimize them, think about a time-chart to guide the days, block out portions, as the summer approaches, remember to call the Salvation Army, remember to donate, strange name, Salvation Army, check the bills, be sure all the bills are done, keep in mind my father's admonition about paying bills on time, continue, navigate all things, write to Royce's aunt Betty, commend her for her fortitude in all things, commend her for keeping the family together, buoyant during hard times, take lessons from those one admires, keep going, keep going, think things through with different emphasis, try different emphasis, juggle ideas in the mind, change priorities, or not, keep them as they are, make lists, like Barthes, what deserves time and what does not, think about time, makes lists, as Sontag did in imitation of Barthes, what one likes and what one does not, get thoughts to the page and move ahead, clear the way, clarity, the long hard road to clarity, walk it, try to pave it, or not, keep ambiguity and uncertainty alive, let them spill into the work, whatever happens, let it take hold, turn to chores when stuck, or not, stay with the work when stuck, most of all, slug it out, June said to draw like a locomotive, steady, with rhythm, regularity, keep the work regular, as a practice, a discipline, a continuity amidst the larger discontinuity, a refuge, a gift, let all thoughts wander towards admiration or wonder, let gratitude take hold, see things as a stranger would, as a foreigner in a foreign land, be taken by difference, let difference continue to be a lure, think about it, sort it out, let it sort itself out, don't labour things, let them come and go as they must, let them take hold, be alert, be quiet, pause and then keep going, take walks, pause, walk again, breathe deeply, allow whatever comes to come.

FORTY-SEVEN

The culmination of a day's work

      the colour green

To imagine the mind in the act of understanding

      a girl in her mother's arms
      her head resting on the shoulder

To shield one another from hurt

      Bach partitas played by Glenn Gould

The smell of spring

      a kiss goodnight
      permission to dream

FORTY-EIGHT

Because we take appearance and illusion for one and the same,
A bounty for the mind's feast,
A pitch for utterance,
Heft for what the eye beholds.

Bending the arc of ideas,
Bending precepts and propositions,
Vacancies and plentitudes,
We thread and unthread the ether.

These stones, under the sun's awning,
Dazzle in greens and blues.
They dazzle in fiery red.
They float and feather down.

Poised for our meditations,
They break in the knowledge of light.
In this extravagant heat,
They vanish and reappear.

Sublime as night is to day,
As horizontals are to verticals.
They bend into vowels.
They shimmer into everything we call by name.

FORTY-NINE

The sky reaches into the imagination as

One listens to a quartet and
Longs to be in the belly of the cello.

One listens to a quartet and
Longs to be in the belly of the cello as

The sky reaches into the imagination.

Like birds repeating their intervallic calls.

FIFTY

Dawn.
The day loosens its long robe,
Swings its door entire.

We have come all this way.

Minuscule anatomies of being.
Speak the sum of one and one.
Here and *here* and *here*.

We have come all this way.

To count them odd and even.
To make a vow for their small bodies.
How they contain the hour.

We have come all this way.

To be in the heart of sight.
As the beating of wings.
As the quiddity of stones.

We have come all this way.

FIFTY-ONE

A large chunk of glacier is breaking off from its mother.

We hear it as far as the Arctic is.
We hear it crash and rumble, numinous as a voice in silence broken.

We take note of what falls, what tumbles.
As blades into a deep wound, shards break the surface of the sea.

The sky sounds its tinny self.
The sky sounds its tinny self.
The dark sublimity of all things slowly comes apart.

FIFTY-TWO

Yesterday, in the sitting room, I heard the thump of a bird hitting the glass window; I saw it lying on its side by the windowpane. Its eyes roamed; its body shivered; its neck lifted and fell in irregular rhythms.

I went outside and sat beside the little creature. It arched towards death, shuffled to its feet, tipped to the side and lay down again.

Suddenly, the bird rose, pushed against the low air and flew off, grazing the grasses, limping through flight, dipping and rising in the diminution of its triumph.

FIFTY-THREE

The extravagance of sight

FIFTY-FOUR

Went the eye snatched from its socket
Tufts of feathers floated on the hedge
Plumes of grey nudged by tiny flies

Went the eye snatched from its socket
A catch for pellets of rain
Gathered in the cup of blindness

Something swallowed the once-seeing orb
The light went down
Into the twisted bucket

Into the cavern
Into an emptiness
Scooped and opened in elegy

FIFTY-FIVE

I write letters to friends. As I write, I take note.

A small bird passes the window.

There are figures on the horizon.
They are lining up and lying down.

To June Leaf:

> *But the birds,*
> *the birdman and the birdlady and the colossal birds—*
> *so calm and still.*
> *I remember when you recalled the pigeon you came upon*
> *while walking down Bleeker Street,*
> *how he, she, seemed so old.*
> *An old pigeon was a strange and fascinating sight. Dishevelled,*
> *awkward. And so too were those wondrous mourning doves*
> *nesting on the air conditioner.*
> *Sometimes, the truth lodged there is too beautiful or too painful*
> *to contemplate.*
>
> *The wind has been fierce and high pitched, screaming its pure*
> *tones through the otherwise quiet landscape. I am moved by it,*
> *by everything. In the middle of the night, the sun still hovers*
> *over the sea.*

I take myself for a walk. The feeling of being immensely pres-
ent, a sense of the enormity of place, the definitiveness of it, its
strong clear beauty. But for the urge to draw, to make something
analogous to the mood, I would wander farther, perhaps feel
safer in my wanderings than I have ever felt before, safe in my
surrender to the landscape, safe in the weathering, safe in the
light.

I take books and pile them on the table. I open one, find a sen-
tence and linger.

Proust:

> *Suddenly, I stood still, unable to move, as happens when*
> *something appears that requires not only your eyes to take*
> *it in, but involves a deeper kind of perception, one that takes*
> *possession of our whole being.*[20]

My mind drifts. I think about Henry James; I could read all the
James novels I have never read.

Or I could learn to draw the figure.

It happens when I am falling asleep—
an idea comes, a phrase arrives,
an image, one that I hope to recall when I awake in the morning.
It never comes back.
I rummage through the rest to find substitutes.

I take note.

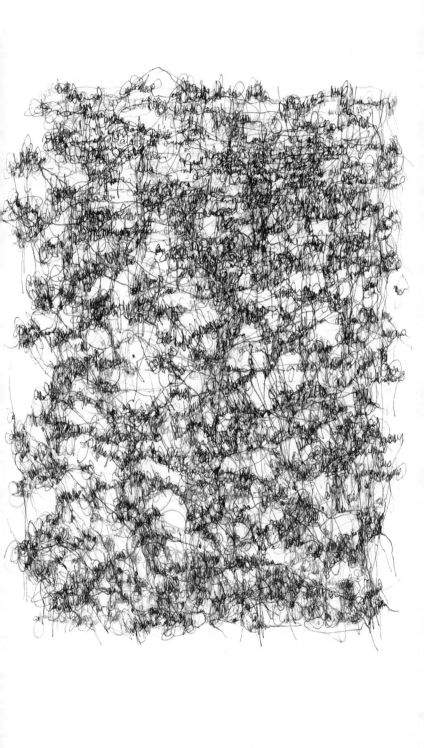

FIFTY-SIX

In the study of logic, the boundary is operational; that is, as soon as we proclaim it as a fact, we refute it on a more essential level. Particles compose the universe; for them, there are no boundaries. They collide; they bounce; they jockey for space; they leap and settle. As their space becomes overcrowded, they push against one another. We call that place of abundance a border, a boundary. Invisible things congeal, collaborate, contest and contrive division. Achille reminds me that what comprises an object is the same as what comprises a country.

> boundary
> a cup of water holds its contents

> membrane
> blood flows through the veins, the arteries

> horizon
> the sea and the sky

> language
> dividing the said from the unsaid

> border
> they try to cross and cannot.

> to fix the categories of thought
> to have these ideas in our linguistic hand

FIFTY-SEVEN

I thought they were band-aids.
The philosopher was gesticulating with bandaged fingers.
He recalled the odium of cats,
How they press against the body.

But, they were fingernails.
They buffered against touch.
It was contact that Deleuze abhorred.
Intolerable the rub of one thing against another.

Intolerable the tips of fingers caressing words,
Marking territories that tremble at their borders.
These inexorable facts,
What separates one body from another.

His nails curled slightly under, as nails will.
They were yellow, as nails are.
They pointed, as they must, at something.
Haptic, ontic and deeply personal.

His boundary would not be transgressed.
It was something.
Not minor, not major
But his own.

FIFTY-EIGHT

East Berlin.
A cold January afternoon.

There is ice on the pavements.
One walks with caution.

Everywhere, artists are at work.

FIFTY-NINE

We enter sideways.

We enter centre.

We settle.

We do it again.

Half-believing

Half in disbelief.

We enter sideways.

We enter centre.

We settle

We do it again.

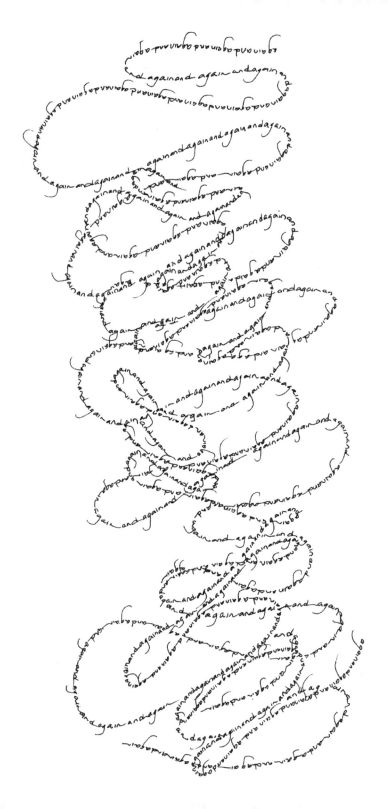

SIXTY

My entry is mid-thought, mid-summer.

Mid.

I enter sideways.

I glean.

Honouring the fallen soldiers of the Iliad,
Alice Oswald imagines their lives, their last thoughts.
I glean.

> *Like when a mother is rushing*
> *And a little girl clings to her clothes*
> *Wants help wants arms*
> *Won't let her walk*
> *Like staring up at the tower of adulthood*
> *Wanting to be light again*
> *Wanting this whole problem of living to be lifted*
> *And carried on the hip.*[21]

I reach for something I can lift to my hip and carry,
something of my own.

SIXTY-ONE

The water is rising

It will spill into drawers
Into pockets and shoes

Books will have their leaves unmoored
They will float through rooms

Their phrases will bob and drown
Scrawled thoughts will fade from the walls

Waves will tumble us
We will be catapulted and tossed

All things will drift to the bottom.

SIXTY-TWO

where
my friend

there
or there

shall we
my friend

find it

too close
too many

here
or there

more
or less

everywhere

my friend
we are tethered

SIXTY-THREE

We wander the earth
We rise with waves in darkness
We fall with stones in daylight
Between arrivals and departures

We are bound and unbound
We ridge the borders
We appear and disappear
Between field and swell

We whisper and are silenced
We open and close our mouths
We name a place that is no place
Between being and not being

SIXTY-FOUR

We walk the hills
Serge and vermilion,

We are some kind of thing
Some kind of human thing,

Some idea
Some kind of possibility.

We tremble the horizon.
We plunge into diction.

SIXTY-FIVE

Time

Spools and unspools the light.

Listen.
A cry festoons the landscape.

Dogs are barking their dark silhouettes.
Their long voices curl along the ridges.

Where are you?

The pen mounts the page.

Listen.
You can hear the air spill over us.

Birds push their desires into the evening.
Mauve and russet, they arch into the weather.

Where are you?

Time

Spools and unspools the light.

SIXTY-SIX

These figures lining the hills
Appear as shapes wrapped in colours.

Oranges and reds.
They are swathed.

Something to behold.
Some kind of human phenomenon.

Some kind of catastrophe.
Something.

1 Gilles Deleuze, 'Literature and Life' in Gilles Deleuze, *Essays Critical and Clinical* (Daniel W. Smith and Michael A. Greco trans) (London: Verso, 1998), pp. 1–7; here, p. 2.

2 Ibid., p. 3.

3 Roland Barthes, *Mourning Diary* (Richard Howard trans.) (New York: Farrar, Strauss and Giroux, 2012), p. 162.

4 Barthes, 'October 31, 1977' in *Mourning Diary*, p. 23

5 Barthes, 'October 27, 1977' in *Mourning Diary*, p. 7

6 Barthes, 'August 1, 1978' in *Mourning Diary*, p. 175

7 Anne Truitt, *Turn*: *The Journal of an Artist* (New York: Penguin, 1987), pp. 5–6.

8 Immanuel Kant, *Critique of Pure Reason*, B374.

9 Ibid., A354.

10 Italo Calvino, 'Multiplicity' in *Six Memos for the Millennium* (Patrick Creagh trans.) (Cambridge, MA: Harvard University Press, 1988), pp. 101–28; here, p. 124.

11 J. M. G. Le Clézio, *The Book of Flights*: *An Adventure Story* (New York: Atheneum, 1972), p. 49.

12 Flannery O'Connor, 'The Peeler' in *The Complete Stories of Flannery O'Connor* (New York: Farrar, Straus and Giroux, 1971), pp. 63–80; here, p. 75.

13 Quoted in James Miller and Jim Miller, 'Be Cruel' in *The Passion of Michel Foucault* (reprint, Cambridge, MA: Harvard University Press, 2000), pp. 165–207; here, p. 169.

14 Jorge Luis Borges, 'The Garden of Forking Paths' (Donald A. Yates trans.) in *Labyrinths* (Donald A. Yates and James

E. Irby eds, William Gibson introd.) (New York: New Directions, 2007), pp. 19–29; here, p. 21.

15 Gilles Deleuze, 'A New Archivist' in *Foucault* (Seán Hand ed. and trans.) (New York: Continuum, 2006), pp. 3–20; here, p. 7.

16 Theodor W. Adorno, 'Lecture Eleven: "Deduction of the Categories"' in *Kant's Critique of Pure Reason (1959)* (Rolf Tiedemann ed., Rodney Livingstone trans.) (Stanford: University of Stanford Press, 2001), pp. 117–27; here, p. 125.

17 Ezra Pound, 'Piere Vidal Old' in *Ezra Pound: Early Poems* (New York: Courier Corporation, 1996), pp. 16–19.

18 Michel Foucault, *The Hermeneutics of the Subject* (New York: Picador, 2001), p. 218

19 Witold Gombrowicz, *Cosmos* (Danita Borchardt trans.) (New Haven, CT: Yale University Press, 2005), p. 133.

20 Marcel Proust, *Remembrance of Things Past, Volume 1* (C. K. Scott Moncrieff trans.) (Hertfordshire: Wordsworth Editions, 2006), p. 148.

21 Alice Oswald, *Memorial* (New York: W. W. Norton, 2011), p. 15.

Deep gratitude to the remarkable
and indefatigable team at Seagull Books.

Special thanks to my son, Gideon Kahn,
and my daughter, Justine Kahn.
Gideon read the text through all its stages,
offering his invaluable comments.
Justine's keen eye and intuition kept and keeps me endlessly alert.

I am grateful to my loving partner, Royce Howes,
who read both the lines and in between them
with his deep understanding of the fundamental challenge
of saying what can hardly be said.

Above all, I thank my precious mother, Muriel,
for her love, her guidance and her encouragement,
year after year after year.